HOW TO START A SIDE BUSINESS

Without Quitting Your Day Job!

Tom Botman

Flourish Publishing

TABLE OF CONTENTS

Introduction: How This Book Will Help You

Part One: Setting Up The Business

    Chapter One: Identify a Good Business Idea

    Chapter Two: Market Research

    Chapter Three: Identify Potential Roadblocks

    Chapter Four: Goal Setting and Action Planning

    Chapter Five: Business Plan

    Chapter Six: Formulate a Marketing Plan

    Chapter Seven: Obtaining the Necessary Capital and Technology

    Chapter Eight: Resources and Setup

Part Two: Gaining Momentum

    Chapter Nine: Managing your Side Business and Day Job

    Chapter Ten: Leverage A.I. and Emerging Technologies

    Chapter Eleven: Scaling the Business

    Chapter Twelve: Leadership and Management for the Entrepreneur

    Chapter Thirteen: Creating Business Rhythms and Rituals

    Chapter Fourteen: Keeping a Positive Attitude and Reaping the Rewards

Conclusion: Get Started

INTRODUCTION

How This Book Will Help You

Do you feel overworked and underpaid, but can't just quit your day job? Are you looking for a way to make more money, but don't have the luxury of risking your livelihood in pursuit of more income? Have you been dreaming of financial freedom, but find it hard to believe you can achieve it without sacrificing your day-to-day security?

If you answered "yes" to any of these questions, then How to Start a Side Business Without Quitting Your Day Job is the book for you. This easy-to-follow guide will provide you with the essential building blocks to getting started in your own side business so you can begin to make supplemental income while still maintaining the stability of your full-time job.

You don't need to be an experienced entrepreneur to start a profitable side business! Whether you have a long-term plan or just need a short-term fix, this book will give you all the tips and tricks you need to get started quickly and reap the rewards without leaving your reliable job behind.
In this book, you will learn how to:

- Develop creative and practical ideas for your side business
- Set goals and create a simple, actionable plan

- Balance your current job with starting a side business
- Manage and prioritize your time
- Choose the right technology to help you succeed
- Formulate a marketing plan to maximize income
- and more!

How to Start a Side Business Without Quitting Your Day Job is an invaluable resource for anyone looking to gain freedom, stability, and financial security. Stop dreaming and start taking actionable steps now to watch your side business grow.

Getting Started

Chances are, if you've decided to start a side business, you already have a basic idea of what that business might be. If so, go ahead and skip chapter 1 which is all about forming a business idea. If you have an idea but not much more make sure to validate your concept through chapters 2, 3 and 4. A strong and well-thought-out business concept will save you lots of time once you are operational, not to mention it can open doors for potential investors, partnerships, or customers and help bolster your chances of success.

Once you have a solid business idea, your first step should be to do market research. This includes researching your competitors, identifying customer pain points, and researching potential pricing models for your services. By completing a comprehensive market analysis, you'll have a clear view of the market's needs and potential areas to position your business in. Additionally, it's essential to consider the scalability of your venture. If your idea proves successful enough, you might want to expand it beyond a part-time endeavor.

Next, you'll want to create a business plan. This document should include your business idea, mission and vision, competitor analysis, and marketing strategies. It should also include an estimated financial budget for startup costs, overhead expenses, and anticipated profit margins. Make sure to be realistic in your projections; it's better to under promise and over deliver than the alternative.

Finally, ensure you have the skills and resources necessary to run your business. Do you need to hire any contractors or freelancers to help? Are there any specific certifications or qualifications you need to possess to practice in your chosen industry? What sort of business license or permit do you need to obtain? Take the time to answer these questions and plan as far ahead as possible to ensure you have the resources and knowledge to run your business effectively.

With your market research, business plan, and resources in place, you'll be far more prepared to launch your side business with confidence. Doing the legwork upfront can set you up for more successful and sustainable business down the line. So make sure you take the time to properly develop your side business idea and enter the business world with eyes wide open!

PART ONE: SETTING UP THE BUSINESS

◆ ◆ ◆

CHAPTER 1: IDENTIFY A GOOD BUSINESS IDEA

❖ ❖ ❖

Welcome to the world of ideation for business plans! There are no one-size-fits-all solutions when it comes to coming up with business plan ideas. Ideas come in many shapes and sizes, and what works for one business might not necessarily work for another. That's why it's so important to be creative and come up with your own business plan concepts tailored to your particular business and goals.

This chapter will provide you with the tools and strategies you need to get the creative juices flowing and come up with your own original ideas. Whether you are in the early stages of launching a business or looking to revamp an existing venture, by the time you finish this chapter, you should have a few inspiring ideas to start with.

Brainstorming

The first step in developing your business plan concept is to brainstorm some ideas. Brainstorming can help you come up with a variety of concepts that you can then narrow down to the best one. Here are some tips to get you started:

Gather your team — If you are in a team participating in brainstorming, make sure all members feel encouraged to share their ideas. Try to come up with as many ideas as possible and don't be afraid of wild or seemingly impossible concepts — you never know what could end up as that big idea.

Journal — Writing down your ideas can help you get a better feel for what you're trying to accomplish and help organize your thoughts. Don't be afraid to start with a blank page and fill up the page with ideas.

Talk to others — Hearing the thoughts of other people, especially people outside the organization, can often be very inspiring. Take the time to talk to others, such as: customers, suppliers, partners, etc, and see if they have any ideas or suggestions.

Mind mapping — A mind map is a graphical and visual representation of ideas, connections, and information. It can be used as a brainstorming tool to create a big-picture view of a project, helping you see something from different angles and perspectives.

Get away from your workspace — You may find it helpful to work from different environments from time to time. Consider taking your brainstorming session outdoors, or to a cafe or any other place where you feel comfortable and relaxed. This can spark new ideas that you hadn't imagined when sitting at your desk.

Narrowing Down Ideas

Once you have a pool of ideas from brainstorming, the next step is to narrow down the selection. This is an important step as it helps you focus on the ideas that are the most feasible, valuable and worthwhile.

Eliminate ideas that don't fit your mission — Any ideas that don't align with your mission, values and objectives should be eliminated right away. Maybe you don't know that those things are yet, then start by asking "Is this something I would like to see exist in the world?"

Prioritize ideas — Ask yourself which ideas are the most feasible and have the best chance of making a positive impact. Once you have narrowed down the list to a few ideas, explore each one in more detail to make sure they are worth pursuing.

Get feedback — Share some of your ideas with others and see what they think. This can help you determine which ideas to move forward with. What ideas seem to get people excited and interested?

Choose the best idea — After considering all the ideas and getting feedback, it's time to choose the best of them. Don't be afraid to throw out ideas that don't seem right and move on to other options.

CHAPTER 2: MARKET RESEARCH

◆ ◆ ◆

Doing market research for a side hustle business might seem like a daunting task, especially if you're just starting out. After all, it can require a lot of time, focus, and planning. But rest assured, armed with the right knowledge and resources, market research can be an incredibly useful tool and ultimately lead you towards success. With that in mind, this chapter will provide an overview of key steps to take when doing market research for a side hustle business — so that you can gain an edge, make informed decisions and reap the rewards.

Step 1: Define Your Product

The first step when doing market research for a side hustle business is to get clear on what exactly you plan to offer. Remember, your side hustle business or product should bridge the gap between meeting customer needs and generating a profit, so it's important that you can clearly articulate the value of what you're offering. Once you have a solid idea of what you're selling and what you stand to gain, you'll have a better understanding of how to conduct the necessary research to prove the feasibility of your market.

Step 2: Identify Your Target Audience

Market research is all about understanding your target audience, so take the time to identify who exactly you're looking to target — including their age, gender, geographical location, income levels, interests, and lifestyles. The more detailed your target audience, the better you will be able to tailor your research and develop a strategy that meets their needs and wants.

Step 3: Gather Market Data

Once you've established your target audience, it's time to start gathering data to inform your decisions. Data is the heart of market research, so do a thorough analysis of the competition, industry trends and customer demographics. By understanding the buying power of your audience and surveying their opinions, you'll be able to get a comprehensive view of your target market and be able to ensure that your product is tailored to their needs.

Step 4: Sources Of Information

When conducting market research, there are many different sources you can use to gather information. Invest time in surveying and talking to real people — such as customers and industry experts — as they can provide invaluable insights and perspective. Additionally, look at industry reports, census information and media outlets to gain valuable insights and intelligence. Be sure to use online resources such as social media sites, blogs and online forums that can give you an understanding of what your potential buyers are thinking.

Step 5: Analyze & Interpret The Data

Once you've collected your data, take a step back and evaluate what it's telling you. Take a look at how the market is changing, how competitors are operating and what people think about their offerings. From there, you'll be able to develop effective marketing and pricing strategies that meet the needs of your target audience.

Don't forget, the information you collect will also be useful when building a business plan. Keep your eyes and ears open and note any key trends, as they can give you insight into the needs of your target market.

Doing market research for a side hustle business is essential, as it will help you gain an edge, make informed decisions and ultimately be successful. Though it may take some time and effort, with the right knowledge, resources and approach, it's possible to do effective market research and be well on your way to success. Hopefully now, you have a better understanding of the key steps to take when conducting market research and are well-prepared to start gathering the information you need.

CHAPTER 3: IDENTIFY POTENTIAL ROADBLOCKS

◆ ◆ ◆

When starting a side hustle, it's important to be aware of potential roadblocks. These could be anything from lack of resources to personal commitments that might interfere with your plans. Identifying these roadblocks in advance can help you anticipate and plan for them before they become overwhelming.

Starting a small business from the ground up can be a significant challenge. While it offers a tremendous potential for growth and financial reward, there are of course roadblocks that can impede its path to success. Recognizing and attempting to mitigate such obstacles as early as possible is often key to the sustainability of your enterprise. Below are some common roadblocks to watch out for when starting your small business.

Limited Capital: Money always plays a starring role when it comes to owning a business. Keeping overhead and operational costs low is key to staying afloat until your business starts to generate a positive cash flow. Start by researching affordable ways to keep your overhead expenses low—like finding a shared workspace or negotiating favorable deals on goods and services.

Execution of Tasks: Businesses require a certain level of organization, and if there is a significant shortfall in that area, it can quickly lead to stalled momentum. Developing a plan for how day-to-day tasks should be handled is vital for keeping the operations of your business running smoothly. Create a clear set of instructions for each employee and delegate necessary tasks to ensure your goals are met on time.

Finding the Right Talent: Investing in the right people is essential for the success of any small business. Employing individuals who have the necessary expertise and dedication can help elevate your business to the next level. Develop a hiring process that weeds out the individuals who are not a good fit.

Inaccurate Accounting: One of the biggest challenges of running a business is keeping track of its finances. If financial records are not accurate, it can cause costly headaches in the form of fines and penalties that could have been avoided with proper oversight. Regularly review financial statements and consider hiring an outside accountant or financial expert to ensure everything is running correctly.

Limited Resources: Working with limited resources is a common challenge for small businesses. Oftentimes, there simply is not enough money and manpower to do what needs to be done. To get around this, look for ways to automate and streamline operations, such as using technology to help with marketing or customer service.

By recognizing and taking steps to mitigate these common roadblocks ahead of time, you can ensure your business is prepared to succeed in the long run. Doing your research and being open to change is key when starting a small business. Once you have the right foundation in place and an understanding of the potential roadblocks, you'll be well on your way to building a successful small business.

CHAPTER 4: GOAL SETTING AND ACTION PLANNING

◆ ◆ ◆

Setting Realistic Business Goals For Your Side Hustle

Having a side hustle is a great way to make some extra money, build new skills and add alternative streams of income. But success doesn't happen overnight. That's why it's important to set measurable and realistic business goals when launching your side hustle.

The best way to do this is to first identify and quantify your ultimate end goal:

Do you want to make a thousand dollars a month?

Or

Do you want to launch your side hustle into a full-time job?

Whatever your end goal is, you need to have a realistic timeline and set incremental goals for yourself along the way. People tend to overestimate what they can accomplish in a short time and underestimate what they can accomplish in a long time. We all want to make passive income with minimal effort, but the truth is that there is effort required and if you set a realistic goal with a longer time horizon of say 1-2 years instead of 1-2 months you will accomplish more in the long term, if you stay consistent.

Another key piece of setting realistic business goals starts with getting honest with yourself and understanding your skill level. Starting a business requires you to wear many hats, so it's important to understand what skills you already possess and what new skills you may need to acquire.

Furthermore, setting realistic business goals takes research into the market you are trying to reach. Ask yourself questions such as, who is my ideal customer? How many potential customers do I need to acquire? What type of pricing should I use? Answering these questions will help you create an actionable plan and set realistic goals.

Finally, once you have set realistic business goals, it's time to start developing an execution plan to reach those goals. Create tasks that will help you get closer to hitting those goals and break them down into realistic timelines. It's also important to get into the habit of tracking your progress and adjusting your goals accordingly. Having realistic business goals will help you focus on the important steps to take to get closer to your end goals. After all, you want to start your side hustle on solid footing and set yourself up for success.

The Goal Setting Process

A successful business is one that is able to bring its goals to fruition. Goals are an integral part of the lifeblood of a business, and it's important to give them the necessary attention and craftsmanship that they require. This chapter serves as a guide for entrepreneurs, executives, and side hustlers on how to create business goals that will maximize profits and propel organizations to the next level.

Before setting business goals, it is important to define a company's mission statement. By ascertaining the company's purpose and goals with clarity, managers and employees will find a focused roadmap to follow. Once the mission statement is established, the process of setting goals can begin. Goals should be formulated with consideration of the company's current and potential resources.

S.M.A.R.T. Goals
S.M.A.R.T. is a common acronym you will find sound goal setting. This acronym really provides an excellent framework for what constitutes a good goal. As you set your goals run them through the smart filter to ensure that you are on track with the right goals.

- **Specific**
- **Measurable**
- **Achievable**
- **Relevant**
- **Timbound**

Specific- Is your goal detailed enough? As an example; "To change the world" is too broad! And you won't know how to gain progress. However, a goal like "Impact hunger by donating 1 million dollars to my local food bank by 2030" now we are getting somewhere. That is a goal you can measure and even find help to do.

Measurable- By keeping track of the metrics associated with the goal, your organization can better evaluate its progress and determine whether or not the goal is achieving what it set out to do. Some common business metrics you may want to consider are: Net profit,Gross Margin, Customer Satisfaction, Employee Engagement, Overall sales, Cost of customer acquisition.

Achievable- No matter how ambitious the goals may be, they should still be sensible. If you are consistently not meeting your goals, it will be discouraging. It is okay to set high goals but start with small ones that build wins in the short run and make your longer term goals more ambitious.

Relevant- Does this goal align with the overall mission and vision of your business. You don't want to work hard for a goal that pulls you in the wrong direction of your overall vision.

Time Bound- Put a deadline on your goal. When does it need to be completed in order to measure if it was successful or not?

In addition, goals should be updated periodically. As conditions change, the goals of the company should also be adjusted. By maintaining vigilance on the goals and monitoring their progress, a business is able to always know where it stands in relation to its objectives.

Finally, business goals should be linked to rewards. By offering incentives for successful completion of goals, employees (or business owners) can be kept motivated and engaged in the business.By creating thoughtful business goals that are realistic, measurable, and linked to rewards, an organization will be well on its way to achieving its objectives. With a clear roadmap and direction, the organization can confidently steer itself towards success.

Action Planning

Creating a plan is essential for success. Depending on your personality you can get as detailed as possible, but I would start with a very simple document that lays out your next steps of action. The details can be added to your Business Plan (see more on that in the next chapter).
Start by writing down the steps that you'll need to take in order to reach your goals. Then, break it down into smaller, more

manageable tasks. By creating a structured plan, you'll be able to focus on short-term goals and track your progress. Follow the key steps below:

Work Backwards: With your goals in mind write out the steps that need to happen to get there. Know that the steps will probably end up changing once you test your product or service and gather real feedback, but with the information that you have now, write out the big picture steps that need to happen. See examples below.

Goals:
Make $1,500/month in profit from my side business
- Steps: Sell 15 courses per month at $100
- Market course to find buyers
- Create and publish course
- Land on platform to use
- Write content for course

Create a course that has high impact and high adoption
- Great comments, ratings and shares of my course
- Excellent material
- Refine user experience of navigating the course
- Test and retest ideas, gather feedback from sample groups to continually refine the content
- Create a MVP (Minimum Viable Product)

Writing an actionable plan for success is the first step to achieving your business goals. By following the steps outlined above, you'll be one step closer to achieving your side hustle dreams. With the right planning and execution, your side hustle won't just be a dream—it will be a reality.

Don't Be Afraid To Get Help

Starting a side hustle can be a lot of work, but you don't have to do it alone. Whether it's hiring a mentor or a virtual assistant, there are numerous people who can help you reach your goals faster and more efficiently.

Have A Backup Plan

Finally, it's important to have a backup plan in case your original plan doesn't work out. Depending on the nature of your side hustle, this could mean having a few alternative strategies or resources that you can tap into. Having a backup plan ensures that you'll be prepared for any unexpected hiccups.

By following these tips, you will be able to create a plan that will help you reach your goals and be successful in your side hustle journey. With clear, actionable goals and a realistic plan, you can make sure that nothing will stand in the way of your success.

CHAPTER 5: BUSINESS PLAN

◆ ◆ ◆

Introduction

As an entrepreneur, you're likely familiar with the concept of a business plan. This essential document outlines the goals and direction of any business, providing a roadmap for success. But what happens when you decide to launch a side hustle?

Having a plan can help you make the most of your side gig and truly use your passion to make a difference. After all, not every business needs a full-fledged business plan. Smaller businesses, such as side hustles, can benefit just as much from developing a written plan that's tailored to their needs and as simple as creating a word document.

In this chapter, we'll cover the basics of writing a business plan for your side hustle. We'll look at the components of a solid plan and how you can use them to make the most of your endeavor.Let's begin by looking at why you need a business plan for your side hustle.

Why Do You Need A Business Plan For Your Side Hustle?

Having a business plan for your side hustle is helpful for a number of reasons. It helps you articulate your vision and goals and serves as a roadmap for your business. It keeps you focused and prevents you from getting sidelined or distracted by unrelated opportunities. It also provides a roadmap for persuading investors, securing loans, and measuring success.

A good business plan should include all of the following elements:

- Your business's mission and values
- Your services or product
- Your target customer
- Your unique selling points
- Your pricing structure
- Your operations, marketing, and financial plans

By taking the time to develop a business plan, you're investing in the future of your side hustle. Plus, it's a lot easier to track progress and spot potential issues when they arise if you have a plan in place.

Developing Your Business Plan

Now that we've looked at why you need a business plan for your side hustle, let's talk about the process of developing one. A good business plan leads you step-by-step through all the key areas of your business. It helps you identify your objectives, think through challenges and obstacles, and develop strategies to maximize opportunities.

To craft a comprehensive business plan for your side hustle, you'll need to include all of the key elements mentioned earlier. Here's a closer look at some of the most important sections and how to approach them.

• **Your Business's Mission and Values** - Begin by articulating the unique mission and values of your business. Brainstorm a list of words to describe your brand, products, and services. Then, narrow it down to three to five core values that will drive your business going forward.

- **Your Services/Product** - Describe the products or services you'll be offering. Include details such as what types of products you'll have, their features, and the problem they solve.

- **Your Target Customers** - Think through who you'll be targeting with your products or services and why. Answer questions such as who is the ideal customer, what problem does your product solve for them, and why will they be drawn to your brand?

- **Your Unique Selling Points** - What makes your business unique or inspiring compared to the competition? Identify what sets your brand apart so you can confidently communicate it to potential clients.

- **Your Pricing Structure** - Consider how you will price your services/products to make profits and compete with the market. Make sure you cover costs, provide value, and offer an affordable price point.

- **Your Operations Plan** - Create a breakdown of the different tasks you'll need to do daily, weekly, monthly, etc., to keep the business running. Be sure to include plans to maintain cash flow, manage expenses, and more.

- **Your Marketing Plan** - Describe how you plan to market and promote your business, including what channels will you use, what kind of budget will you have, and what message will you communicate? (More on this in the next chapter)

- **Your Financial Plan** - Create a detailed plan for how you will finance your business, including sources of capital, budget for expenses, revenue streams, and cash flow projections.

As you craft your business plan, remember to be flexible and revise it as needed. This is especially true when it comes to financial planning. The costs of supplies, services, and labor can all change quickly, so it's important to adjust your plan accordingly.

Moving Forward

Now that we've covered the basics of writing a business plan for your side hustle, you're ready to get started. Developing a business plan doesn't have to be a daunting task if you take it one step at a time.

Start by outlining your goals, vision, and unique value proposition. Then, break down the operational and financial aspects of your business to create a detailed roadmap that you can use to track progress and measure success.

By creating a well-thought-out business plan for your side hustle, you'll have the resources you need to build a successful business and make your dreams a reality.

CHAPTER 6: FORMULATE A MARKETING PLAN

◆ ◆ ◆

Starting a side business requires that you create a solid target market and a viable marketing plan for your services. Your target market is the specific group of people you'd like to reach with your business and services. With the right target market analysis and marketing plan, you'll get the most bang for your buck and be able to ensure that your side business reaches its full potential.

Marketing Strategy

Let's start by taking a step back and functionalizing the concept of marketing strategy. By definition, marketing strategy is "a plan for reaching the desired objectives for a business, product, or service. This plan typically incorporates market research and encompasses decisions on product, pricing, positioning, and promotion." So, marketing strategy is the route you take on your marketing journey to meet your desired objectives.

Target Market

Now, let's move on to how to define your target market. Your target market must include customers who are most likely to buy services from you. To do so, you need to consider both demographic and psychographic characteristics. Demographics can include gender, age, income level, industry, job title, and location – anything that involves information about your target customer. For psychographics, consider the values, activities, interests, and opinions of the consumer (i.e., what motivates them).

Outreach Efforts

Once you know who is in your target market, you need to come up with a plan to reach them. Your marketing plan should include tactics to build awareness of your side business (Social media accounts, signage, posters, business cards, paid advertising.), how you'll promote your services to your target market (In addition to the things listed above, think about the look and tone of the brand you are creating). Include a process that verifies customers are satisfied (survey, customer service email etc.) and come back referring you to others (business cards, referral rewards etc.). Next provide opportunities for ongoing relationships with customers (email list, follow on social, promotions etc) , and how you will measure your progress.

Cost

When creating your marketing plan, there are a few key pieces to keep in mind. First, consider the cost of each marketing activity. Before selecting an activity, make sure the cost is within your budget. Also, consider the time it will take for each activity. It might be a great idea but if it's not feasible given the time you have, look for alternatives. Additionally, think about the value each tactic can provide to your side business. The better the return on your investment, the higher the value to your business. Make sure to market your products or services at the places your customers will see. For example, online ads through social media sites or web browsers may be great for an online course but may not be as valuable if you do bike maintenance in your garage in a rural area. In this scenario, it may be better to utilize free online resources (bike forums, social media groups etc.) first before committing your precious capital to ads.

Results

Finally, measure the performance and effectiveness of your marketing plan. This is important so that you can adjust your plan and make improvements where necessary. Pay special attention to what is working and where there is room for improvement. This is an important step and will help you make sure your side business is on the right track. Consider tracking some measurable results such as marketing to sales conversion ratio or guest satisfaction score.

Starting a side business is exciting and overwhelming, but with the right strategy and target market, you can be successful. By understanding defining your target market and forming a marketing plan, you can ensure that your side business reaches its full potential and makes a lasting impact. Taking the time to understand and craft a strategy that meets the needs and interests of your target market sets your side business up for success.

CHAPTER 7: OBTAINING THE NECESSARY CAPITAL AND TECHNOLOGY

◆ ◆ ◆

Starting a side business is an exciting and profitable venture. But in order to make a successful start, entrepreneurs need to have the capital, technology and support resources necessary to get their business up and running.

Fortunately, there are a multitude of funding opportunities available, depending on the nature of one's side business. Entrepreneurs can apply for business loans, line of credit, venture capital, and various other forms of public and private funding. Many of these funding options come with terms and conditions, and in most cases require some level of equity in the business.
The decision to enter into a venture capital relationship should be approached with caution. Venture capitalists are looking to invest in up-and-coming businesses, and those applying for this type of funding will need to prove their potential for success. This can include a well-thought-out business plan, solid financial projections, and access to resources for the side business.

While most businesses nowadays require some kind of technological infrastructure in order to run efficiently, this is especially true for a side business. By having the right technology in place, entrepreneurs can easily manage their day-to-day tasks, maintain communication with customers, and minimize the risk of running into any potential problems.

Some examples of technology entrepreneurs may need include:

- **Web hosting services** – To access your website, customers will need a hosting provider.
- Business planning software – To plan operational tasks, budget, and timeline.
- **Customer Relationship Management software** – To effectively manage customer relationships, build loyalty, and track sales data.
- **Cloud storage** – For automated data backups and secure file storage.
- **Point-of-sale systems** – To carry out simple and efficient transactions.
- **Accounting and tax software** – To help manage finances, taxes, and billing.

In addition to technology and finance, entrepreneurs should also consider other resources available to help them get their side business up and running. This includes things like employee and freelance support, industry mentors, business networking, and marketing resources.

Overall, having the necessary capital and technology is essential for any aspiring side business. With the right resources in place, entrepreneurs can be sure to have a successful start.

CHAPTER 8: RESOURCES AND SETUP

◆ ◆ ◆

Preparing To Launch Your Business

Now that you've got the foundation of your business in place, it's time to focus on the details of preparing to launch. The first step is to make sure that you have the right resources and skills to run your business effectively. This means taking the time to answer important questions like:

- Do you need to hire any contractors or freelancers to help?
- Are there any specific certifications or qualifications you need to possess to practice in your chosen industry?
- What sort of business license or permit do you need to obtain?

Answering these questions and planning for the future can help you stay organized and prepared to run your business.

The next step is to think about the specific skills and knowledge you need to operate your business. Evaluate the current skills and resources you have, and then identify any gaps that need to be filled. Depending on your industry, you may need to acquire specific certifications or licenses. It's also a good idea to reach out to professionals, like lawyers and accountants, who can help with compliance and other business needs.

Choosing A Business Entity

When it comes to choosing the type of business entity, there are numerous options available. From LLCs (limited liability corporation) and sole proprietorships, to corporations and S corporations, each carries a unique set of benefits that must be taken into account.

LLC's-To start, let's examine LLCs. A limited liability company offers the business owner significant protection from individual liability. This means that any lawsuits, debts, or other financial obligations cannot be tied to the owner's personal assets. LLCs are easy to form and maintain, and are often the preferred choice of small business owners.

Sole Proprietorship- Next, there's the sole proprietorship. This type of business entity is owned and run by a single owner, and is the simplest form of business entity. It offers fewer legal protections, but is simpler to form and maintain. This structure is suitable for small businesses that don't require significant capital or formal structure.

Corporations- both C and S corporations, offer several key advantages over LLCs and sole proprietorships, including liability protection and the ability of several investors to pool their resources. Furthermore, these entities offer far more flexibility when it comes to issuing stock and attract better hiring talent, as these entities are viewed as more established and reliable.

When it comes to deciding which type of business entity is the best fit for you, it is important to take into account the amount of protection and capital investment needed, as well as the desired structure of the business. Carefully considering the pros and cons of each business type, in comparison to the business goals and objectives, is paramount to the success of any business endeavor.

Seeking Help

The nature of a side hustle means you are probably building your business or secondary income stream on your own however you may need to bring in additional support to move things along faster. Consider hiring contractors or freelancers to help in areas where you don't have the necessary skill set. Hiring the right people to support your business can help you scale quickly and efficiently achieve your business goals. Make sure to carefully interview each candidate to ensure they have the right experience and qualifications as well as the right cultural fit.

Finally, think about the resources you need to properly run your business. Do you need access to capital? Are there any specific software or equipment you need? What about the office supplies and other amenities you need for your team? Asking the right questions and planning for the future will help you ensure that you have everything you need to make your business successful.

We hope this chapter has given you insight into the task of preparing to launch your business. Gathering the resources and skills you need to succeed is a critical step in setting yourself up for success. If you take your time to answer the important questions, plan ahead, and set yourself up for success, you'll be well on your way to achieving your business goals.

PART TWO: GAINING MOMENTUM

◆ ◆ ◆

CHAPTER 9: MANAGING YOUR SIDE BUSINESS AND DAY JOB

◆ ◆ ◆

Are you ready to explore the vast potential of starting and managing a side business? The idea of having an additional income stream that helps to pay the bills or allows you to move toward your long-term goals is a dream come true. And while many people worry that a side business is just a pipe dream or a waste of time, there are plenty of success stories out there to show that this extra effort can pay off.

Managing a side business, however, is not a walk in the park. When combined with a full-time job and family obligations, working on a side business can quickly become overwhelming. The key to success is having a strong plan and developing effective time-management strategies.

Here are some tips to help you manage your side business and day job:

1. Set A Schedule: Develop a schedule that outlines when you will work on your side business and when you will focus on your day job. This will help you stay organized and ensure that you don't run into any time-management issues.

2. Prioritize: Understanding what tasks are urgent, what can be done in the short term, and what relies on a longer turnaround plan is an important part of effective time management. Prioritization allows you to focus your efforts on the most important tasks that need to be done first and foremost.

3. Set Deadlines: The key to successful time management is to set deadlines for yourself and to stick to them. Having a timeline in place will ensure all work activities are completed on time and that nothing falls through the cracks. When setting deadlines, make sure to allow for some margin of error, as the unexpected can often occur.

4. Outsource: If you're really struggling to find enough time to work on your side business, consider outsourcing certain tasks. This can include anything from social media management to website maintenance.

5. Delegate: Once you've established a team to help you with your side business, make sure to delegate tasks appropriately. Having clearly defined roles and responsibilities for each team member will help ensure that everything runs smoothly.

6. Automate Tasks: Automating tasks such as customer service, marketing, and billing can save you time and help you focus on more important tasks.

7. Take Breaks: Don't forget to take breaks throughout the day. A few minutes here and there can make all the difference in keeping your focus and productivity up.

Managing a side business and day job can be a daunting proposition when you're first getting started. If you keep these tips in mind and develop a plan that works for you, though, you'll be in a great position to build a successful side business.

CHAPTER 10: LEVERAGE A.I. AND EMERGING TECHNOLOGIES

❖ ❖ ❖

In today's competitive business environment, leveraging the latest technology and tools is essential to staying ahead of the competition. Artificial intelligence (AI) and emerging technologies offer a wide range of opportunities for businesses to increase efficiency, reduce costs, and gain a competitive advantage. This chapter will discuss how leveraging AI and emerging tools can help build a successful business.

Ai And Automation

AI and automation are two of the most important tools for businesses to leverage when looking to increase efficiency and reduce costs. AI can be used to automate tasks that would otherwise require manual labor, allowing businesses to focus on more important tasks. AI can also be used to improve customer service, as it can be used to respond to customer inquiries quickly and accurately. Automation can also be used to streamline processes and reduce the amount of time and effort needed to complete tasks.

Data Analysis

Data is one of the most valuable resources for businesses, as it can be used to gain insights into customer behavior and preferences. AI and emerging tools can be used to analyze large amounts of data quickly and accurately, allowing businesses to make better decisions and gain a competitive advantage. AI can also be used for predictive analytics, which can help businesses anticipate customer needs and trends.

Marketing

AI and emerging tools can also be used for marketing purposes. AI can be used to create personalized ads and content that is tailored to individual customers' needs and preferences. AI can also be used to analyze customer data to determine the best strategies for reaching potential customers. AI can also be used to optimize campaigns and track performance, allowing businesses to make more informed decisions.

Conclusion

Leveraging AI and emerging tools can help businesses increase efficiency, reduce costs, and gain a competitive advantage. AI can be used to automate tasks, analyze data, and optimize marketing campaigns. By leveraging AI and emerging tools, businesses can gain insights into customer behavior and trends, allowing them to make better decisions and stay ahead of the competition.

CHAPTER 11: SCALING THE BUSINESS

◆ ◆ ◆

Introduction

Scaling a business from start-up to enterprise is a daunting task. It requires careful planning and execution to ensure success. There are a number of challenges that come with scaling a business, such as finding the right resources, getting the right people in place, and managing the growth of the business. This chapter will provide an overview of the key steps to scaling a business from start-up to enterprise, including the importance of developing a business plan, finding the right resources and people, and managing growth.

Working The Business Plan

Previous chapters discussd the importance of a business plan and how to create one. Working through that plan will keep you on track. Refer to it often and continue to make progress on the vision that you set from the beginning. The business plan should also include a detailed roadmap for the business, including milestones and goals. This roadmap should be regularly updated as the business grows and evolves.

Finding The Right Resources And People

The next step in scaling a business from start-up to enterprise is to find the right resources and people. This includes finding the right suppliers and vendors, as well as the right employees and partners. It is important to ensure that the resources and people are capable of meeting the business's needs and can help the business reach its goals.

Managing Growth

The final step in scaling a business from start-up to enterprise is to manage the growth of the business. This includes managing the financial resources of the business, as well as managing the operations and processes. It is important to ensure that the business is able to handle the increased demand and that the business is able to scale up quickly and efficiently.

Conclusion

Scaling a business from start-up to enterprise is a challenging process. It requires careful planning and execution to ensure success. This chapter has provided an overview of the key steps to scaling a business from start-up to enterprise, including the importance of developing a business plan, finding the right resources and people, and managing growth. By following these steps, businesses can ensure that they are able to successfully scale their business and reach their goals.

CHAPTER 12: LEADERSHIP AND MANAGEMENT FOR THE ENTREPRENEUR

◆ ◆ ◆

Introduction

Management and leadership are two important concepts for any entrepreneur. Management is the process of planning, organizing, leading, and controlling resources to achieve goals. Leadership is the ability to influence and motivate others to accomplish a goal. While these two concepts are often used interchangeably, there are important differences between them. This chapter will explore the roles of management and leadership in the success of an entrepreneur and provide strategies for successful implementation.

The Role Of Management

Management is the process of planning, organizing, leading, and controlling resources to achieve goals. It is the process of efficiently and effectively utilizing resources to achieve desired outcomes. Management is critical for an entrepreneur because it helps to ensure that resources are used effectively and efficiently to achieve the desired outcome.

The Role Of Leadership

Leadership is the ability to influence and motivate others to accomplish a goal. It is the ability to inspire and motivate people to take action. Leadership is important for an entrepreneur because it helps to create a vision, develop strategies, and build relationships with stakeholders.

Strategies For Success

There are several strategies that an entrepreneur can use to ensure successful management and leadership. First, it is important to set clear goals and objectives. This will help to ensure that resources are used efficiently and effectively. Second, it is important to develop a plan of action and make sure that everyone involved is aware of the plan. Third, it is important to delegate tasks and responsibilities to ensure that everyone is working together to achieve the desired outcome. Finally, it is important to provide feedback and recognition to ensure that everyone is motivated and inspired to reach the goals.

Conclusion

Management and leadership are essential for any successful entrepreneur. It is important to understand the roles of management and leadership and to develop strategies for successful implementation. By setting clear goals, developing a plan of action, delegating tasks, and providing feedback and recognition, an entrepreneur can ensure that resources are used effectively and efficiently to achieve the desired outcome.

CHAPTER 13: CREATING BUSINESS RHYTHMS AND RITUALS

◆ ◆ ◆

Establishing Routines For Success

Routines are an important part of success for any organization. Establishing a daily business rhythm and incorporating rituals into it can help an organization to stay on track and progress towards reaching their goals. This chapter will provide an overview of the importance of establishing quarterly goal setting, annual reviews and rhythms of celebration for businesses and will offer suggestions for incorporating them into existing routines.

Quarterly Goal Setting

Setting goals each quarter is important for any organization to stay on track with their progress. It is also important to recognize that goals should not remain the same throughout the year: they should be revised if necessary to reflect the changing needs of the organization. Having regular goal setting meetings allows organizations to review their progress and once a quarter allows them to adjust their strategies accordingly.

Goal setting meetings should include all pertinent stakeholders, such as managers and employees. This allows everyone to be involved in the decision-making and allows everyone to provide their unique perspectives. In addition to setting goals, it is important to discuss strategies for achieving them and identify any potential challenges or roadblocks that may arise.

Annual Reviews

Annual reviews are an important part of any organization's business rhythm. Annual review create an opportunity to look at the entire year of performance. This creates space to celebrate wins, as well as set new priorities based upon new objectives for the upcoming year. This reflection time ensures that the business doesn't become stagnant, it is another opportunity to highlight the progress you made toward accomplishing your vision.

In addition to a business review the end of year is also a great time to evaluate employee performance and provide feedback for individual progress. An employee review allows for transparency between a managers view and employee view of progress made and alignment with culture. It also allows for employees to be held accountable and create plans for additional development to help them achieve their career goals.

Rhythms Of Celebration

Finally, it is important to incorporate rhythms of celebration into the business. This can be done through organizing activities such as company picnics, staff retreats, parties or awards ceremonies to recognize employees' successes. Celebrating individual or team successes helps employees to feel appreciated and motivated to continue to work hard. It also allows the organization to acknowledge and reflect on the progress they have made towards their goals. Even if you are working as a solo entrepreneur on your side hustle, make time to celebrate. If you hit a financial goal or your business operated for its first year, celebrate those milestones.

Creating business rhythms and rituals is an essential part of any organization's success. It is important to establish routines such as quarterly goal setting, annual reviews and rhythms of celebration to ensure that progress is being made and goals are being reached. By following these guidelines, organizations can ensure that they are setting themselves up for success

CHAPTER 14: KEEPING A POSITIVE ATTITUDE AND REAPING THE REWARDS

◆ ◆ ◆

Despite being in a fledgling stage, starting a side business can deliver long-term rewards and great satisfaction. It is important, however, to equip yourself with the right attitude, so you can make the most of this opportunity and reap the rewards of your hard work.

Remember The End Goal

One of the best ways to stay positive is to focus on the bigger picture. Setting goals that you can achieve in the short, medium and long term is a great way to keep your enthusiasm high. When you map out the steps needed to achieve these goals, you can focus on taking one step forward at a time.

Learning to delegate tasks especially when all the names are completed can be challenging but also liberating. Delegating tasks to staff members, interns, or contract workers can lighten your own workload and allow you to take the time to enjoy the success of the business. Moving forward, delegation will be a key to the success of your side business.

Enjoy The Process

It's also important to set aside some time for yourself, even when things get busy. Carve out an hour or two each week to read a book, watch a movie, go for a walk, or do whatever it is that brings you joy. This will not only help you recharge, but it will also be a reminder of why you are doing the hard work in the first place—to experience more happiness and fulfillment in life.

At the same time, you should take the highs and lows in stride. Don't expect success to come overnight and don't get too down on yourself when you encounter setbacks. Things don't always go as planned, but it's important to stay persistent and know that it's all part of the journey.

Finally, it's essential to keep your physical and mental health in check. Prioritize regular sleep, exercise, and healthy eating. Surround yourself with positive and supportive people and take steps to stay organized and productive. All of these things will help foster a sense of energy and enthusiasm that is contagious and an important part of staying motivated.

Starting a side business is an incredibly rewarding experience, but it takes more than just hard work and tenacity to make it a success. Having the right attitude and habits and staying motivated throughout the process is essential to your long-term success. When you equip yourself with all the right tools, you will be well prepared to reap the rewards of your hard work.

CONCLUSION

Get Started!

You have now reached the conclusion of How to Start a Side Business Without Quitting Your Day Job. By now, you should have a better understanding of all the steps necessary for success when starting a side business without quitting your day job.

The most important piece of advice here is to start today; not tomorrow, or next month, or next year. Take the time to research, plan, and implement your side business. With the right amount of preparation and diligence, you can gain the traction and success you need to take your side business to the next level.

By getting out of your comfort zone, taking risks, and remaining resilient and flexible, you can also accomplish something truly remarkable. Working hard, being determined, and never giving up will lead you to the places you want to go.

There are a lot of steps outlined in this book but the most important one is the next one! Just keep moving forward, do the first thing within your power today. Remember your goals and aspirations of owning your own business. With the right attitude, dedication and commitment, you can be your own boss and move towards building a prosperous side business that will ultimately lead to financial freedom!

www.ingramcontent.com/pod-product-compliance
Lightning Source LLC
Chambersburg PA
CBHW031533210526
45464CB00014B/2790